Crossroads To Clarity

How a salesman found his

smile again!

By Dario Cucci

831 DESIGNS UK

831 Designs is part of Forever Family Forever Free group of Companies whose address can be found at 831designs.com.

First printed in the United Kingdom by Amazon

This book was created using the You Speak, We Create done for you service at 831 Designs.

First published 2017
831 Designs
London. UK
www.831Designs.
com

Book: Crossroads to Clarity
Dario Cucci. -- 1st ed.
ISBN-13: 978-1981143061

ISBN-10: 1981143068

For Tanya

Wish you the best
of Health + Success,
to you.

[signature]

Foreword

I first met Dario Cucci when he attended The Public Speakers University and straight away I could see that he was a determined man on a mission. He had a clear idea of what he wanted to do and so I thought that his intense look was because of his focus, little did I know ….

As Dario was became a member of The Professional Speakers Academy I was able to spend more time with him on a one to one basis. It was here that he started to share his story and of course this is when I first learned about his Bells Palsy and so I realised that he struggled to put a smile on his face, not through lack of happiness it was in fact as a result of this "frozen face".

Getting to know Dario over the 6 months that followed showed me how he was determined to make sure that both his clients and their customers received a great service. It was apparent that his love to serve others was of primary importance from the professional slides of his presentation to the level of service he wanted to provided that would wow them. As a student he pushed himself to the limit and completed the course in a record time, the reason was because he wanted to get out to share his message and that is exactly what he did.

Even when he had another attack of Bels Palsy which rendered him almost speechless, he still showed determination and balls of steel (a northern term!) and he went ahead and spoke at an event because he didn't want to let the promoter or the audience down.

It was clear to me that he had found his WHY! which was to inspire others (as the co-founder of The Find Your WHY! Foundation (http://www.findyourwhyfoundation.com) I help people to find their WHY as in their passion and also how to understand WHY they are right now in their lives (the good things and those that could hold them back)

At this stage I wanted to help Dario in this case not with his presentation. I wanted to help him to get his smile back and as a qualified Rapid Results Transformation Therapist (RTT is a hybrid of hypnosis, N.L.P & therapy created by Marisa Peer) and so I knew I could help him to understand WHY the Bells Palsy was returning and holding him back.

After just 1 session the change in Dario's face was literally uplifting and the muscles were able to move and post a quick adjustment to a recording I made for him he was indeed able to smile again. We were able to recognise that it was those times in Dario's life where he felt out of balance that the Bells Palsy showed up and so armed with this information Dario was able to take back control and focus on his passion.

I believe this is what makes him unique as a Sales & Service Coach that helps Business Owners with their mindset and communication because he know what happens when the mind over rules the body and how it feels when you don't have the ability to communicate.

Now he has his smile back he is able to help others to smile too ☺

I recommend Dario to anyone looking for an authentic coach to help them in their business.

Dr Cheryl Chapman C.Hyp RTT

'LIFE IS NEVER EASY IT HAS IT'S
CHALLENGES AND YET ONCE WE
EMBRACE THEM WITH OPEN ARMS
LIFE CAN BE BEAUTIFUL BEYOND
OUR OWN EXPECTATIONS'

DARIO CUCCI

Contents

'KNOWING YOUR PURPOSE IN LIFE IS A GIFT WHEN YOU ACCEPT IT, IT'S A WASTE WHEN YOU IGNORE IT!'

DARIO CUCCI

CHAPTER 1

The Wake-Up Call

It was lunch time, I was feeling so unhappy, I was so close to resigning, my limits had been pushed, I had put on weight, I was stressed, I had anxiety, this was due to the fact I was compromising my own integrity.

All of a sudden, I felt my face change…

All of a sudden I couldn't speak properly…?

I didn't know where it came from or what was happening to me?

At first, I thought, "Maybe it's just momentary." And it would disappear, but it didn't…?

I told the manager "I think I've had a stroke?"

That's when the ambulance collected me,

Emergency lights from the office to the hospital, I was all alone laying on a hospital bed.

Not knowing what was going to happen.

They took my blood, they did an MRI of my brain, and they analysed everything…

Those three hours were the longest three hours of my life!

I didn't know what was happening with my health, Will I see my family again?

Will I die here all alone?

Than a feeling of regret set in and I started asking myself a different question...

Have I lived my life with purpose?...

I had not lived my life the way I had planned and dreamed. I was lying there, I was asking myself, "Have I lived my life with purpose? Have I really done what I set out to do?" The answer that kept coming back to me was, "No, you haven't."

In that moment in time I had lots of pictures in my mind, images going through my brain, I saw myself on stage inspiring and educating people, watching people getting excited about what I had to share. That is how I finally realized what my purpose was, in that moment, that time. Behind the fear and Panic came the greatest gift of absolute clarity for me and my life's purpose.

Over the years I worked in the self-development industry, one of the things that angered me the most was the cutthroat industry, how it's being handled and managed. At the front end everything is glamorous and great and at the back end it's all about getting the numbers right and not really looking after customers in the best way possible. I never really liked that because I believe that the customer is a person, they are not a number, every time I had to sell a program, or I had to hear complaints from people, they felt they weren't looked after. I felt bad for them because on one hand I wanted them to succeed, on the other hand I still needed to go and do my job. A few times I clashed with the CEO and management heads because of this issue.

My health took a turn, I put on weight, I was stressed, I had anxiety, this was all because I was compromising my own integrity, doing things that I didn't agree with, selling a program, I knew that if people weren't applying themselves correctly they wouldn't get any value from it. Or that the program that's being sold at the event wasn't really working, they were told to believe that, and I wasn't allowed to tell them otherwise. I had to literally swallow my pride and be quiet about it even though I knew, people were investing into forex mentoring program that wasn't working and that people lost money instead of making money as was always promised.

The day when I was rushed to hospital, I was having lunch, I felt I wasn't really happy, I was very close to resigning from my position at that time. I had been pushed to my limits. All of a sudden I felt something change in my face. I couldn't really pinpoint what it was, it was almost like a crack kind of effect happening. I felt my face changing. All of a sudden, I couldn't speak properly, and I didn't know where it come from. At first, I thought, "Maybe it's just momentary." And it would disappear, but it didn't. So, I went up to the manager and I said, "I think I had a stroke." That's when an ambulance delivered me, emergency lights from the office to the hospital, where I was laying on a hospital bed. Not knowing what's going to happen, they took my blood, they did an MRI of my brain, and they analysed everything, those three hours were the longest three hours in my life! I didn't know what was happening with my health, will I see my family? Will I not because all my family are in Switzerland? At that time, I was in Australia. So, I knew that if there were anything to happen to me, I wouldn't be able to just go and leave to see them. The biggest fears that I had in that moment was, will I die? And will I not be able to see my family again? Then I became overwhelmed with a type of regret, I had not lived my life the way I had planned and dreamed. I was lying there, I was asking myself, "Have I lived my life with purpose? Have I really done what I set out to do?" The answer that kept coming back to me was, "No, you haven't."

In that moment in time I had lots of pictures in my mind, images going through my brain, I saw myself on stage inspiring and educating people, watching people getting excited about what I had to share. That is how I finally realized what my purpose was, in that moment that time. Behind the fear and Panic came the greatest gift of absolute clarity for me and my life's purpose.

Now let's go back before this occurred, I was previously pursuing my dream of becoming an actor, I studied acting the Meisner technique at The Actor's House in Sydney for almost five years, I had written my film script, which I planned to star in and get the producers to buy.

I did this alongside selling a lot of mentoring, and coaching programs, NLP trainings with Chris Howard, Tony Robbins, other mentoring programs like James Schramko, Kerwin Rea and Jamie McIntyre. I then moved from Sydney to Melbourne. In Melbourne it changed, I didn't do as much acting, but I still was pursuing acting. I truly believed I was born to be an actor. It was at this time I realized that acting was no longer fulfilling me. An actor does what he's told to do, he's just another employee, you're not allowed to have an opinion. You must only be your character in the way that they tell you to do it and that's it. You are not allowed to think for yourself, they tell you to just be.

I did both acting and sales. My sales job at this time, was for other people, I was building everyone else's business, and not my own. This was not my purpose. This was somebody else's purpose that I was living, I lived somebody else's dream, I helped them make serious money, while I was an employee that barely made any money, or commission. There was no security in this, the last job I had in a position like that was 20,000 Australian Dollars and then the rest was commission. They offered me another position where I got more than 50,000 a year with less commission, it was just not rewarding. It was never my purpose.

The reason I was working for somebody else, was always with that goal in mind that one day I can go to the United States, go to Hollywood, work as an actor, create the dream. Now when I remember that, I'm wondering "Why did I think that?" It doesn't make sense to me anymore because I'm a very opinionated person. If somebody upsets me I tell them. A director once pissed me off, I told him. I ended up losing a job because of it, but I still stand by it. I can see myself as a speaker, because as a speaker I am a leader, I'm not a follower, I'm actually a leader that inspires change in others, were as an actor, you're a follower, the actor is the last person that they hire before they start a film. Everyone else, including the director or the cameraman is hired before that. The actor is the last person hired, (unless they're known, of course.) If they're known, it's a very different story. In this industry, they are the last person. They are very easy to replace because there's such a high competition out there, if you don't work hard they get somebody else. They don't wait around for long. So if you are losing your job, there are a hundred or a thousand people in your place that want to take it.

As an individual person, as a speaker, as a leader, there's only one Dario. There's no-one else like me. I want to be that person that transforms and inspires change.

I really gained this awareness when I was in hospital, when I was on the hospital bed. I mean, I studied a lot of self-development. I was always learning, I did grow from it and I was aware. My ego was telling me, "I want to do acting." I kept telling myself that, it almost clouded my vision in that sense, it never allowed me to really ask the tough questions... if I were to die today what legacy would I want to leave behind? What is legacy? Is it a Hollywood movie? Not really. What is my legacy being, if I were to die that I know that my name and what I have taught people lives long beyond me?

The people in customer service, for instance, are so brilliant in holding conversations that they not only make sales, they get the customer to really feel like they're appreciated and leave them with a smile. They remember that smile. Instead of being angry and frustrated that they have been put through all those different agents and issues. That is what I want people to remember, I want people to remember that the customers should always leave with a smile, and for my legacy purpose I want business owners and companies to start changing their attitude and start really taking an interest in people and treating people as individuals, not as numbers.

This will take time, and courage because what I am telling people to do is to listen and to adjust and adapt instead of just going with a cookie cutter system that everybody else uses. I am even going as far as challenging the customer when they are telling you bullshit. To really go, "So is that really what this is about or is there something else beyond that?" You can only serve people when you are asking the right questions, not staying on the surface, go deeper to the real goals, what is real in your heart?

Now how can you gain your awareness?

I do not wish anybody into the shock, or illness or hospital to get their awareness. I don't think it's a fun thing to do. There's a lot of things you can do to get awareness as I did. From, overcoming my fear of heights down to doing meditation, self-hypnosis, NLP, past integration, which is part of NLP and being hypnotized, that's continued growth.

Now, one of the things that you need to be willing to do, to discover and have the awareness called your purpose is you need to let go of the ego. Let go of thinking who you think you want to be or what other people think you should be. All of that is stripped away because the essence of purpose, and I'm not talking about what's your purpose of getting a job done, I'm talking about the essence of your purpose, why you are born in this lifetime, that is very deep, that's ingrained, that's a blueprint that is given to you before you were even born. It is given to you by a higher power, or by God, whatever it is that you believe. It's your task that's been given to you before you were born. So, whilst you are in your mom's womb, you actually have that as a job to fulfil after you're born, and you grow up. You just don't know it yet. It's in the subconscious level, it's like deep, deep, deep ingrained. So, what needs to happen is you need to go through all the frequencies, ideas and conceptions of who you should be or shouldn't be, and you need to listen to your inner voice, if you want to call it that, or let God guide you, whatever you prefer to call it, it's ultimately within you. You need to just listen to it. And that takes time.

The reason that it came to me was because I was in a situation where I felt I might die. As I didn't know at the time, why did I have a stroke? Is there a blood clot in my brain that is causing this? Is it something else? Could it be more severe? So, in that moment I was in uncertainty, so I wasn't thinking, "How much will this bill cost?" Or "What am I going to do about my face when I don't look as good anymore."
Nothing superficial. I was very clear," Now let's just let go of all the bullshit that I made up around me and within me and ask the question, if I were to die today did I really truly live my purpose?" When I asked myself that question from a place of just being myself, it came to me, without forcing it. It didn't come to me through story or anything, it came to me through pictures in my mind visual pictures that I saw.

Everybody has a different way of processing, some people hear a sound, they hear a voice, or they hear a word, or they get a feeling and it really depends on what your primary drive is in the way your subconscious communicates with you. Sometimes for people it's the sound or people are looking at more, they're more visual, perhaps for those are pictures. There is no right and wrong, it's just the way it is. The best way to get there, (instead of getting ill) You can meditate on it, you can write out all the emotions and everything for hours on end, until it comes to you. It's not a very practical kind of thing to do because, again, the ego plays tricks on you when do stuff that is ego-driven, and writing is egodriven. "Oh, my writing isn't that good." "Oh, I made a grammar mistake." All that is ego. So, the best thing for anyone to do is get to a state of mind where you can let go completely of the ego.

That is the best way, it might take more than a moment, it might take years for people to get there, you know because the ego is something that we are brought up with. So, to strip off the ego and let go of everything is very difficult for people. Meditation is good, and even getting into, something like, yoga, do that on a regular basis and eventually it might help you get to that place. Or just switch off all the lights and just lie down and add some relaxing music and then meditate with the intention to let subconscious guide you to your purpose. Ask yourself, "What I am born to do in this lifetime? What's my purpose?" And then just close your eyes and relax and let it come to you. You aren't trying to force it, whatever happens, happens. It might happen, it might not happen. Do not give up. I tried all these things, still it was never clear until that moment in hospital. For me, that was my journey to discover.

Activity 1:

Take 15 Minutes out of your busy Day and sit down to answer the following Questions.

1. Have I lived my Life with Purpose fulfilling myDestiny?

If your Answer to that Question is "NO" then you need to ask yourself.

2. What needs to happen for me to be living my Lifewith Purpose and fulfil my Destiny?

Write out everything that comes to mind, that needs to happen for you to get there.

Then ask yourself the last Question.

3. Am I ready to commit to Change and do whateverit takes to make it happen?

If the Answer to that is "Yes" then get in touch with me and let's hold a Conversation, to how I can help you achieve your Goal to build a Business with Purpose, following your Destiny. Email me: admin@on-call-business.ch

Subject: Clarity Consultation Call.

Activity 2:

Focus Daily when getting up on what you Bring to the People you meet to be of Service and attract more Abundance.

To do this, close your Eyes, tap into a positive Emotion and then announce to yourself the following Affirmation:

I Bring Love

I Bring Knowledge

I Bring Experience

And at the end of saying that, you say out loud, I Bring It!

Until you feel you are ready to start the Day.

And at the end of your Day, write out 3 – 5 Things you where Grateful for, before going to sleep. This will totally shift your Focus and help you make positive changes in your Life.

'TO CHOOSE YOUR

DESTINY YOU HAVE TO LET

GO OF THE PAST TO

FINALLY HAVE CLARITY.'

DARIO CUCCI

CHAPTER 2

Clarity

Clarity for me is a challenge, because I am so creative, I always have ideas, I get a lot of thoughts all the time. Clarity was one of the biggest challenges that my brain had because an entrepreneur always thinks of ideas, how he can improve something. When I got that clarity that I'm not supposed to build someone else's business up, I'm supposed be a leader instead of a follower, it was really difficult to commit to that because I needed to literally quit my job, and move back to Switzerland.

As a result, I ended up, working for someone else just to get back on my feet again, and to get a routine again. Though it was a distraction, it wasn't something that satisfied me, I realized I cannot be like this anymore. It's not healthy for me, so clarity came, again, through being stressed, being in a job that I didn't enjoy anymore because it felt the same as before. I was literally prisoner to the system. "You're paid to do this, you're paid to do that." Anything else other than that you're not allowed to do, you must do certain things, even if you don't agree with it you still need to do them because you are employed.

Even when you know it's not working, sending out emails to the masses to invite people to have a conversation with you, that's not going to work. It just doesn't. You're better off calling people and then hold a conversation and see where it takes you, rather than sending out emails to try and book an appointment, then calling them to make an appointment because they're just going to avoid doing that and it takes a lot of time to chase them.
You would have, in half the time, made more sales.

I was working for a marketing company at the time. They created chocolates with edible greeting messages on the chocolate that was made from sugar. They would be sent to the companies who would buy credits to then create those chocolates themselves with their logos and slogans on and we would send it out. When I did my thing, within one week I made 12 sales. When I did what my boss told me to do, who's the CEO of the company, we didn't make any sales for three weeks. Not one. because it just took too much of our time to do it the way that he wanted to.

I told him it's not going to work. Three weeks later he asks, "Why isn't it working?" I had told him why it's not working, because it's just too cumbersome to create an email template, send that out, then call them, then see if you can make an appointment and then they ask for another email to send the information, when we could have avoided all that and just called them, tell them, and then send an email. That's much more efficient than the other way around.

That's when I got the clarity, I don't want to work for anyone that's incompetent anymore. If somebody's incompetent, they can pay me to become competent, then that's a different story. Then I am telling them what to do instead of the other way around. That's when I had complete clarity. That's when I created my company "On Call Business". At first, I thought of, providing a service for health professionals but I changed that over time because I felt it's not working, it's not worth the time and money because then they don't have time or the customer doesn't have time and I gave that up and then I had a conversation with one of the guys from Bums on Seats and when he brought up, "Why don't you, hold your own events?" I started thinking about that, and that's when I got clarity that public speaking is actually what I really Love to do.

Funnily enough, as I went through to the training to attend the Jet Set Speaker system where Andy Harrington did all the training, the more I did all that, the more I gained clarity how I wanted to do it. I learned his system, but I figured out I want to do more than the system, I want to do it my own way. I ended up attracting clients from the U.K much more than from Switzerland where I lived. So, I started building my business in the U.K, holding seminars and a master class. I ended up guest speaking at other events like the Power net event, or the Laptop Lifestyle Bootcamp and I was guest speaker at two of the Bums on Seats workshops during the lunchbreak and I sponsored the Power to Achieve event twice, I did that to get my name out there and the more I ended up doing that the more I got clear about what it is, and how I wanted to live, how I wanted to serve people and that is how I gained my clarity and then as a result of it I got some really great results with those people that started working with me.

You must get rid of what holds you back, and let go of your past.

For me, saying is acting for me still a priority or not? Then when I made the decision it's not, it was letting go of the past. That's it, finished, do I enjoy it? Yes. Will I still do it? Maybe as a hobby or maybe I will use it as skill set when I present? For me letting go of the past also meant not looking back at all the mistakes I made in the past, including wrong investments when I lost a hundred thousand dollars in Australia when the market crashed because everything looked good for like two weeks and then the market crashed. All the investments that I had lost all the money I could have had. For a long, long time I felt guilty about that. At some stage I said to myself, "I need to let go of that, I can't hold on to that anger because it's not productive." When you hold on to guilt, it is counter-productive in the way you grow because everything is affected by it, touched by it. So, I went back, I forgave myself for having made the wrong investments. I didn't know that the market was going to crash, that is a risk that's there when you do investments it was a lesson, that's just the way it is. There's nothing that I could have done or anybody else could have done. The market crashed, and I was one of those people that had to suffer from it and that was my learning. Learn to grow from that, that's it. What I learned from it, this was a growing curve. Not to give up and keep on going, which I did.

I think letting go of anger against other people. Against my acting teacher that once made a real nasty comment, I had to let go of that, I had to forgive him. Forgive him for being immature, of not knowing how to handle a person's dream when those dreams are shared. Just accept that I shared a dream with him without ridiculing me and that's it. Apparently, at the time, he wasn't mature enough to do that. So instead he humiliated me in class. As a result, I didn't go back to him anymore. In the meantime, I let go of that, I learned to let go of that, I forgave him. I forgave myself in the sense of how I reacted to it. Those things needed to happen in life, you need to let go of anything that's pulling you down. Because only then you can have clarity to move forward. If one foot is in the past and one is in the present wants to go into the future, you are stuck, you'll not move forward into the future because if that one foot is in the past, it's like mud holding you back. It's like you're walking through mud and there's this big mud clay on your foot, holding you back. As soon as you let go of it, you can easily move forward and walk the way into the future the way you see fit. That is the best way to do it.

Then for me all those things I've done, forgiving myself, the first thing that I say to people about it is, "Forgive yourself for all the mistakes you have made." The decisions that you made in those moments were with the knowledge and the resources you had at the time. No human being goes into this world asking, "How can I fuck up my life the best possible way?"

Our intention is normally a good one. Human beings generally have a loving blueprint. It comes from love. We fuck up because we think we want to take a shortcut or we know better or we think it's a great opportunity and then it turns out not to be. We couldn't know that at the time. So, this is where, the first thing you need to do to is let go and forgive yourself. For all the mistakes. And instead of looking at it as being a mistake look at it as it was a learning curve, it was feedback showing you can grow better.

That's more positive, that's more empowering. Ask yourself a question, "What from that bad experience was the positive learning that I can take away from this? So, then you can forgive yourself." You ask yourself that question, then it will be easier to forgive yourself.

The next step is, instead of reflecting on the past in a negative way, look at one or two learnings that you can take from it that can drive and motivate you forward. The third thing that you can do is, instead of living in the past, by that I mean there are people out there who talk, "Once upon a time when I was this age, this and this and this." Well, guess what? You're now 40, 50, 60 years of age, you're not 20 anymore, it's not a go back in time kind of thing like Michael J. Fox. Go back to the future. You are here in the present and now. So why not just focus on the now instead of the past or the future?

Eckhart Tolle wrote a great book called "The Power of Now". He says, "When you are living in the now, there are no regrets, because there is only now. And every now is a now. And then from that now you create the future." But you have no idea how the future will be created because your presence is in the now. Philosophically speaking, the subconscious mind is in the now.

The subconscious mind is like a child. I say it's like a child that wants to learn. It's always yes. A child doesn't say no, it's a preconceived idea to say no to something. A child that is, say, anywhere between five and seven, or even, you know, five and ten, they say yes to most of the things. They hardly say no. The reason they say no is because they learn to say no by watching what the adults do. In the beginning there's always, "Do you want to know what this is?" "Yes." "You see this is on the floor?" "Yes." "Can you smell that?" "Yes." And it's always yes. That's why even little kids, for instance, they literally crawl on the ground on the floor anything they find they put in their mouths and smell it and touch it, do whatever. Then you get a ten-year-old and he says, "Oh no that's something that's ugly I'm not going to pick that up." But how does a ten-year-old know that it's ugly? Well, it's because his parent or society told him, "That's ugly, don't pick it up." Now, it's a shit on the floor, a ten-year-old will not pick up the shit, while the three-year-old will just go into it and then smell it and feel like, "Oh, it's not good." And then leave it. But the first instinct was, "Yes." "Yes, I want to discover what this is. Is it shit or is it chocolate?" Don't know, so let's have a look.

If we have that level of curiosity and we learn like children do, we can grow so much more in life and we can enjoy our life so much more because it is just in the now, and then we appreciate the now much more than we start to think about the past and the regrets that we have or think about what the future might hold and be fearful that we can't achieve it.

Be present in the now. Then just listen to your heart and really come from a heart place. Ask yourself, "If you reflect on your memory-" and your memory is an illusion, by the way. Some things you will never remember so you'll, make stuff up, because there are certain gaps. If you ask yourself the question, "What do I need to know to forgive myself and others?" Coming from a heart place, and then you close your eyes, and you let those thoughts take you back into that what you just asked, "So what do I need to learn to let go of the anger and sadness and forgive myself?" Then when the subconscious mind shows you that you can than say thank you so much for the learning and then just come back in time and apply that learning to every event, asking the subconscious mind, "Now apply this learning to every event." That's one way of letting go of anger or sadness or any kind of negative emotions.

The simplest way to really forgive yourself is to make the decision to forgive yourself. To just say, "I forgive myself for what happened." And then if you need to vent the anger or sadness, one exercise you can do, is say, "So, what is the biggest learning that I got from this experience and what do I need to specifically learn to forgive myself? What do I need to learn to forgive the other person? And what emotions do I need to let go of to forgive myself?" You write those questions down and then you start writing, writing, writing the answer until it doesn't make any sense anymore. And it doesn't matter how much you write. If it's a page, four pages, or more. And it's not about the order, it's more about venting the emotion by writing. So, what will happen is, eventually when you keep on answering those questions and writing out the emotion and how you feel about it and the situation that you want, what will happen is, you will, because of it, you will neutralize the emotional attachment. Because all of a sudden you are starting to realize different points of view. because you're not looking just through your eyes, you are asking how can I forgive that person? Why did they do this? Then start writing it all out. Suddenly it neutralizes the meaning of it.

Another powerful thing to do once you've written out all of that, you get a metal bucket or something that is fireproof, you put all that paper in there and you light it all and, you let it burn. So, by letting it burn you ask the universe around you to take care of it. To let it go. So, you let that entire thing, all the negativity that you projected onto that page, anything that was negative, you'll let it go and you'll let the universe help you letting it go. By burning it. And then all the ashes fly into the sky.

CHAPTER 3

Integrity

I worked for many companies, some of them had great integrity or they had the intention to have great integrity and others didn't. One thing that I found was, that in the companies themselves when there's more than like 10 to 20 people and you start having different departments, then integrity becomes really, confusing. I'll give you an example of integrity. No naming names but let's put it this way: the company would say, that I worked with and sold event tickets to and all that, you know, if you sell this today, you can offer it to a person for £3,000 as an example, I was in Australia at the time and then the supervisor would tell me, or manager would tell me, "Well, you know, you can give $500 less if they make the payment in full today." Then I ask, "Is that the best price that we can do?" And they say, "Yes." So, I give the program, the membership or whatever it was for two and a half thousand. Although that's great, that's a great deal for the customer. One week later, we see the marketing department launching an online marketing campaign saying, "By the way, you can get the same program for only 997 with monthly payments of £97. So, all of a sudden, I was looking like I was in the wrong, that in the sales department we didn't know about that promotion that marketing had, and all of a sudden, we looked like the liars because we sold the same program one week before for two and a half thousand. More than double the price. Almost triple the price.

That's an issue that I don't like in general about companies, that they have the different departments and all of them have different rules, different campaigns and different ways to deal with it, instead of working with one another, it goes against one another. And it's very stressful because then you, as the salesperson look like a fool. I believe marketing should enhance sales. Some people will not buy online, they need to speak to somebody. When the salesperson knows what is online on offer, the salesperson can talk to the person on the phone and sell it. Or even go as a basis from there and upsell them into something bigger. But for that to happen, it needs to happen with integrity.

So, companies quite often lack that integrity because of miscommunication. Not because they have bad intentions, it's more miscommunication between the different departments that lead to that lack of integrity. The people then think, "Well, I bought this for 2,500 but I could have gotten it for like 1,000 and they wouldn't give me a refund, no way they would change it, I will never go and do business with them." Or they might say, "You know what, they ripped me off." And so, suddenly, the customer has a bad taste to having had dealt with that company. And it could have all been avoided if the company would have better communicated and been all on the same page with every department and every employee to deliver value and sell their service and products with integrity on every level.

For me, integrity also had to do with me seeing that happening and not being able to change it because I was employed and that was one of the things that stressed me, that I literally put my life into someone else's hands. I gave part of my life away to literally sell other people's products and I wanted to do it with integrity and yet at the same time, I had to compromise my own integrity because of the setup that they had and because of what was happening behind my back. Where people didn't do the right thing. It wasn't always done with integrity and then you need to decide for yourself. For me, for instance, whenever I sell something, including my services today, I only sell what I believe in, I only take on clients if I believe I can help them. I don't want to be in the situation anymore where I sell anything or recommend anything without having integrity, because that's a real core value to me.

Even if I give a referral to someone, I will do it from a place of heart because I believe in your service and I experienced a good service and that comes from a place of integrity. Now what you do with that customer, if that customer is being looked after or not, that's yours to deal with and I, for my part, have done everything with integrity. If the other people don't do that, that's on them. My recommendation for any entrepreneur and business owner is know your values, know how you want to be of service to your customers and when you grow, make number one priority to communicate that with your customers and be there for them at all the times. Don't take that for granted and instead what you can do is reach out to them, ask what you can do there, ask how you can be of better service and if they give you feedback, take it on with thanks. Instead of being defensive about it, and show them your appreciation. You do that, people will stay with you even if your prices aren't the cheapest. If your prices are in mid-range and the competition is a bit cheaper, if you show appreciation to your customers and you do it with integrity, also meaning that if you say that it's a special deal that it is a special deal, if they don't act they miss out on the special deal. It's as simple as that.

I say to people when they come to my seminar, "If, at the end of the day you want to work with me, the offer that I am making is for today. Not for whenever." if they come back later, they didn't take up the offer, and they come back two weeks say, or a month later or whatever. The offer has changed. It will be more expensive, or it won't be with all the bonuses etc… That is because I always want to do things with integrity.

The breaking point for me was, I called this guy and asked him how he enjoyed the seminar because he attended the seminar that was a multi-speaker event and he said he enjoyed it, but he didn't enjoy the experience he got from buying the program, because he paid his pension money, he paid about $5,000 to learn internet marketing and how to make money at it. Now, prior buying it he went up to the speaker and asked him, "Is this something for someone like me? I have never done anything like internet marketing?" The speaker told him, "Yes, it is." After him saying that, he signed up and paid with that. Now during the five, six weeks when they did the training, even the expert, the assistant emailed them. The expert's assistant wasn't helpful because the language that they use was more advanced and they used words like hosting or domain name and keywords and, you know, things like that. For him those are all new words, he didn't get it, he didn't understand what is hosting. He didn't know what they meant when they said, "You need to find your niche and then find a product in that niche that you think can sell online with blogs." He couldn't get it and he asked for a refund.

Instead of doing the right thing with integrity in that moment, the speaker refused the refund because it was a few days outside the refund period. One week outside of the refund period. But they guy complained throughout the weeks that he was unhappy. The service, he's not happy, content, he doesn't get it, and then instead of accommodating him they ignore that, and they didn't deliver on the value that he picked for. When I spoke with him he said to me, "This is money that I got from a pension I really want to get it back, now." Then I went to the account manager and they refused to do that, and they said, "Well, it's not because of us, it's because the speaker refuses." So, I spoke to the guy again, and I said to him, "Look, let me help you." I explained to him what hosting is, I explained to him what a domain is, I explained to him how he can write articles about fishing on like, a blog, and WordPress and then use one of the products that is out there to promote it as an affiliate and make money. So, I explained that in great depth to him and after half an hour talking to him he said to me, "Dario, I've learned more from you in this half an hour about what you explained to me than over the last five, six weeks of this expert that I paid $5,000 for. So, even if I didn't

45

get the money back, I appreciate that you made the time available to help me with this, I really do." And again, for me, it was integrity. If it would have been up to me, I would have approved that refund in that case, speakers like that do that because all they see is the money and they don't care about the person. And if they don't care, they shouldn't be a speaker. If you don't want to be a leader, don't be a leader, be an employee. Don't just be a leader to make a lot of money and then leave your customers hanging in the balance, that's notice.

CHAPTER 4

Finding Answers Beyond The Living

I compromised myself because I wanted to be loved. That's the ultimate thing. When you're not secure in yourself, you want to please others, so they acknowledge you more, and then as a result, you end up compromising how you love yourself. That's where I say "Well, I used to have relationships with people where they've literally humiliated me. They didn't appreciate me," and even in the work field, the same thing. I would always be the person that gives the most and then be undermined or overlooked.

Being promised three times a promotion in my lifetime and then I've been given a promotion just to be taken away when I didn't behave the way they wanted me to behave. Twice, it was said, "Oh, you've almost got it, but you didn't," and that hurts because you think, "Well, I'm doing everything that I can and yet, you still don't love me." I mean, that's how you see it. It's just crazy because in my eyes, what is love?

Ultimately it has to do with other people loving you. I mean, what is it about you loving you? How has it ultimately affected your everyday life from partnerships down to doing the business that you do because ultimately what ended up happening is I didn't love myself. So, what did I do? I overcompensated for wanting love from other people in every way and I would literally put everything on hold, even compromise how much contact I had with my family.

Ultimately, I made some money from it, but it didn't get me anywhere and the relationships where not long-lasting relationships. There are some people who you have long-lasting relationships with and they are the ones that you would hold onto, but me I had relationship after relationship that were not longlasting because at the end of the day, I was giving so much of myself that it compromised everything, including my health and now these days, to be honest, I mean, it sounds arrogant, but to be honest, I don't care if people love me or not. I really don't. It's like if you love me, great. If you don't, you don't.
That's it.

I mean, do I want you to hate me? No, I don't want that, I do want people to respect who I am and what I do and accept who I am, yet at the same time, I'm now at a place whether it's private or business, I will speak my mind. I will be myself and either you respect, accept or love that or you leave it and that's it. So, there's no in-between anymore and I don't feel like I need to go out of my way to the 9th degree to please everybody so they'll love me. It took me a long, long time to get there.

I came to that realization about love for myself, recently and that, even though I came to that realization, I need to accept and love myself as I am, it's still a working progress. This is me. I can see and be, stand up for what I believe in and who I am as a person, I will automatically attract the right kind of people that will love me for who I am without having to expect me to be a certain way or do certain things for them.

I used to be the exact opposite. I had relationships in business where I was literally going out of my way to please business partners, employees to make sure that they were pleased with me and if they didn't, I would take it personally. I'd say, "Well, why didn't this person appreciate who I am and why did that person didn't value who I am and all that?"

The same goes in a relationship privately. If you're in a relationship and you come home and the person doesn't acknowledge you because they're deep in thought, you might take it personally and say, "Why doesn't this person acknowledge me?" When in fact, they might just be in a different world. They might be thinking about something different. It has nothing to do with you, but you see it as you.

One of my mentors and coaches that I'm working with right now said to me, "You need to accept that regardless of how people perceive you to be, don't take it as an attack towards you. Don't devalue yourself because of their reaction, according to their world and how they see you, because it has nothing to do with you. So, when people pay you, they pay you for the service and the value that you deliver, but it hasn't to do with your skills, why they aren't paying you as they value who you are and what you do. It just means they're in their own world, possibly struggling in finances or possibly they are going through distractions and that is why they do that and do behave that way, but don't take it personally."

For a long, long time I used to take it very personally when people ended up paying late, not being on time, things like that and the thing is, I came to the conclusion right now that it has nothing to do with me and for me, for me personally, as a coach and mentor, I right now say, "My prices are this. If you want to work with me, you work with me. You'll understand that here's what I'm asking for or you don't," because the last thing that I want to do is chase people for money because I cannot focus on coaching you as a client if I have to chase you for the right payment that you owe me because then I become the bookkeeper. Then it becomes that annoying relationship of me reminding you of the bill. You cannot really coach someone doing that.

Now you can hire somebody or even get somebody to do all that and I don't want to do that because my belief is that in exchange for my experience and knowledge, I want clients that do not blink an eye when they hire me. They understand the investment. They value my experience and they pay whatever I'm asking for. They see it as an investment. They can deduct it from their taxes if they want to. Ultimately, I coach, mentor and show them how to make more sales and I come from that place of giving you all my experience and knowledge and telling you how to practically apply it immediately in business.

I'm not going through so many other agencies and experts or you need to first fill out a 20-page sheet on analysing all the details, asking you 100 questions down to the nitty gritty where you think, "Oh, my God. Didn't I just answer that?" On page 16, "Oh, yeah, I did, but it was in a different way." You'd think, "It's so much paperwork, I don't know where to start and where to stop." No, with me, you are getting practical experience that you can apply immediately.

When you are caught up in the admin, you cannot serve people because admin is paper. Paper doesn't care. I mean, paper, you can write anything on the paper. It doesn't care what it is that you write. The meaning of what we write on the paper is the meaning we give it, but the paper and the ink that's on the paper, it can be anything. Doesn't mean anything ultimately and if you're focused on paperwork in your business, you will not make money.

That is why I say in every business, sales are the heart of every business and so is customer service, but we need to care more about people instead of numbers. So, for me, love has a lot to do with loving your customer as they are, and taking them by the hand and asking, "Who are you? What is it that you want to achieve and how can I help you?" The biggest task for me is to know are they ready to be helped. Some customers aren't. They want to be in their troublesome world. They want to distract themselves. Some customers want to make life difficult and they aren't ready, but when the customer is ready to work with you as a coach or as a consultant or whatever it is that you do, then ultimately, it needs to come from a place of love that you are wanting to serve that customer.

Do not compromise your own values, instead align yourself with that person and say, "Here is my experience. This is how I can help you," be yourself and still value who you are and be confident in who you are and what you can do for that customer because one of the things that the customer wants is that you are confident. If you're not confident, why should anybody invest in you if you're not confident? If you say, "Oh, I've got a service, but I'm not sure if it's the right thing for you." Then of course the customer doesn't buy. If the customer doesn't buy because they've got their own excuses, don't worry about it. I get them all the time. In one ear in, and out the other.

The thing about that is for me, love has to do with loving who I am and what I do all the way through in every area of my life and are there things to improve? Absolutely and at the same time, you are yourself, I came to accept and love myself even with my weaknesses, one thing that I learnt is when I start with knowledge, my weaknesses, I can work on them. I can make them my strengths, but the only way that I can change is if I acknowledge and love and respect myself for where I am. I cannot go back into the past and say "Oh, I should have done that," because the past is the past, and I cannot go wishful thinking into the future, saying, "I wish I had this," because it's not yet created.

The only thing that I can really do is just focus on right now. What I've learned is that this is a lot easier. Since I've been doing this, since I've been focusing on just the now and being in the flow and serving people with love, I attract the right kind of customer and I believe in that. I believe I attract the right kind of customers. I attract the right kind of people that help serve people in the business industry. I attract the right people to help me get my name out there and it is so much easier then when I used to try all the things to do that logically should work, but then didn't, and why? Because sometimes I'll have this little thinking, "Oh, if I work with this person or I'm following this person, they will help me get there."

I was disillusioned because I wanted it so much, when you want something so, so badly and you are the only person that wants it so badly, but the person that you hire who really doesn't care that much or where you're going because they've already got your money. So, you paid them three, four, five grand and now they have got your money and you want it and you are going after it. If you're not getting anywhere and the empathy and the really caring attitude that gets you there, to stay in touch with you when you're not doing it right is not there. The thing that I really don't like in the industry of self-development is that people, some experts in the industry don't care enough for their customers. If you get that a person has not been in contact with you in two or three months and they're a client that pay maybe 5,000, 10,000, 20,000 pounds, the least you can do is pick up that freaking phone and ask, "How are you doing?" that does not hurt you one bit.

If you are doing just that and then listen to what it is that they need, then you can serve them better and that love and experience that I have, I want to share it with the world. I want to transform the world of industry experts to show them how it's done. I want to kick their freaking asses and get them to wake up to themselves and say, "Hang on, I can actually do this. I can serve my customers better," because I don't need to have an assistant to make those phone calls. I can do that phone call myself and even if it does take longer, I can always say, "Look, let's book it in," and then you take charge of that customer and you book them in for a proper session when you do have the time, but you know what? It will transform the world.

I don't know who came up with that bullshit title of customer service or customer support. Instead to be inventive is a happy customer consultant because in all honesty, customer support or customer service is not a service. All they do is basically read, through the terms and conditions and tell you what can and cannot be done. That's not a good or helpful service because what you're really doing is telling people the limitations. Now tell me, if you have a car and you go to garage and they say, "You have four tyres. Alright. Let's put a hole into one tyre and then we will ask you how we can help you," is that a service? No, it's not. It's actually damaging.

What do we do? We buy something and then there is a limitation on the device or the app and instead of solving the problem, they tell you that they cannot solve the problem, but they knew about that problem. They just didn't mention it until it occurred to you and that is the problem. That is the issue with companies and customer service in general and that is where I am different. Yesterday I called somebody, and I knew that she had been going through a rough time and I just called her because I texted her. I emailed her and there was not much of a response from her for whatever reason. I called her, and she took the Skype call and we had a chat. Then out of that, I said to her, "Why don't we do a healing session?" Today I have a healing session with her.

After the healing session, I said to her, "So how do you feel now?" She said, "Well, it feels like I just reset my system to start fresh and I feel cool and that's good." I said, "That's good. That's good. That's exactly the intention that we had because you were so overwhelmed with thoughts and what's going on from the past that you needed to reset your system. Otherwise, you're just too caught up in it." That was exactly what she wanted. Now, I could have done this over two months ago with her, but the customer also has a responsibility to respond. If you're reaching out to a customer and they don't respond, for whatever reason, you cannot mind-read, but for whatever reason, I didn't hear from her for like two months even though I invited her to all the things that I did. I took the phone to make that phone call.

Now, did I put time aside? Extra just for that? No, I didn't. I just did it. When I had a minute, I did it and

I think these days, love in business is missing because people are too caught up in business and in life with what they need to do, instead of living their purpose, instead of being aligned and in connection to people, they are so caught up doing the right thing, that they completely forget about the connection with the other person, the ones that trusted them, that gave money to them. We need to change that. We need to reconnect with people. We need to build a relationship. My belief is once you come from a place of love and not being money greedy, but just love and care, then things will work out and the people that for whatever reason cannot afford your service, I believe that once they're ready to work with you, they will find a way to make the money or they will get the money somehow to work with you.

If they're not ready, then they don't want that. So that's okay too. There's nothing wrong in that. Then you've got space for people that are ready to work with you and do their finances to show their appreciation, in exchange for what you do for them. So, for me, love has a lot to do with it, your own love, my own love. The love that I feel for myself. I am the only person that I know of that has a dark sense of humour and can still smile even when he goes through tough times and keeps on getting up, keeps on standing up. Even if things are challenging, I keep on getting up, I keep on pushing through. I am not only resilient, but I'm very stubborn in some ways. So, in that same time, I'm very flexible and adaptable and caring and all those qualities I do love about myself.

There are not so good, and I love them too because, guess what? Can I improve my cleanliness at home? Yeah, absolutely I can, but it doesn't mean because I have that that I hate myself for it or that I judge myself or put myself down. I don't do that anymore. I used to. I don't do it anymore. For me, love's all about accepting who you are in your life at the time of your life because then you can truly transform and attract the people that you really want to attract into your life. Then you can share the love with other people. If you are at that place of loving yourself as you are, you can also share that love and grow from it, because there's no negative emotion attached anymore or no negative expectations that you need to fulfil or some things that you need to do. So instead, it's all coming from a level place.

CHAPTER 5

Auntie Ursula

My favourite auntie. Her name was Ursula and one thing that I loved about her was every time you would visit her, she always was bubbly, warm, and caring. You would never suspect that anything is wrong with her or anything is going on. For me, she was literally like a warm soul. I remember every year when we went to visit her, she would make those beautiful apple quiches, that I would enjoy. She baked so well. She was really caring. I mean, for me, the one thing that I remember is the quiches that she made and the way she was caring and warm. There wasn't one bad hair on her, always be there for anybody, really unconditional love.

For about four years, I did jazz dance classes and I remember one day coming home from jazz dance and having dinner and I had a feeling something was wrong, and the phone rang, and my mom took it, she came back. She said to me, she needed to go to see her brother because, my Auntie had killed herself with sleeping pills and alcohol.

I didn't go to the funeral. I wanted to remember her as I had her in mind. For me as a teenager, I thought, "If I go to the funeral now, I will remember that as my last memory. I don't want that." Over 30 years later, I did a healing and we did do an exercise, a healing session with one of the other participants and connected with the ones that were passed on.

I asked to be connected to her and the thing was when that happened the other person would hold my hand, they would close their eyes. They go to level seven, where God is, asking for her and she would turn up and they described her because when a person passes away, their soul continues to live. So, they will eventually move on. They get a new task, they get reborn and when you ask for them to come onto the seventh level, where God is, they will actually come, but the way that they come and show up is different than what you have in mind. So, the person described her as this big, big heart talking. I could see that, and I was seeing that, that big heart talking and then I spoke to her, and I ask her, "So why did you kill yourself?" She said, "because it was time for me to go."

Then I said, "Are you okay?" She said, "Yes," and then she also said, "Dario, whatever you are doing right now, in regard to your business, keep on doing it. You're doing well. Keep on persisting on it." I didn't even ask her about it. She just told me that. I didn't ask, "Are you proud of me?" Or anything. I was just asked, "Are you okay?" Then she said, "Yes, I'm fine. I'm at peace and all is fine." Then she said, "keep on going. People will hear you and all will be ok". That for me gave me real closure, you wouldn't believe because for a long, long time, I was worried that she was hurt, that she was really broken and when she said, no, she was fine. She was ready to go, and it was okay, for me, that was my closure.

I said, "Are you happy?" And she said, "Yes all is, fine." That is the only thing that mattered to me, that she is happy. No matter where she is. That she was looking down on me, knowing what I'm doing and even encouraging me, showed me how much she cared. She showed that caring, loving person even beyond the grave. Then later, I spoke to my mom, I told her the story of what happened during the Theta healing session and I asked, "Why would she say that she was ready to leave when she was only 50 years old?" My mom started to share all the stuff that happened in the past that her husband cheated on her with another woman, that the kids moved out when they were adults and she felt not needed anymore and I said to her, "Why did you never tell me all of this in 30 years?" She said, "Well, because we never really brought it up." So, for my mom, it was forgotten about, but for me, it took 30 years to get closure because it was always in the back of my mind. I never understood why someone feels they are ready to go, but after my mom told me that, it made even more sense to me.

I think what we need to learn in life is to really become more transparent and communicate with one another, no matter if it is in this lifetime or if it is on a different level and the person has passed on, because I believe if we would learn to even communicate beyond the grave, to connect with the love ones that passed away, which I know is a gift when you can do that. It will make things so much easier for us, because then we can literally let go of things because we tend to hold on to tragic things, but we don't have closure for years and years and it affects everything in our life, including loving ourselves.

THERE ARE ENTREPRENEURS THAT

DREAM OF A BETTER LIFE AND THEN

THERE ARE THOSE THAT MAKE

THEIR DREAMS BECOME REALITY

WHICH ONE ARE YOU?

DARIO CUCCI

CHAPTER 6

Discovery the Real Me

I was always good at selling. When I did sales in retail or even as a waiter, I was always one of the best. I would always end up getting more tips or selling extra supplements at a retail store. When I was personal trainer, I did in the first ten days or so, I sold about 14 trial packs, because I told them, "It will give you results," I needed the money and within two months, I ended up being booked out 30 to 40 hours a week, making really good money as a personal trainer and I stopped personal training after about four and a half, five years and after that I got an offer to work for a team in Australia.

The job was commission based on its own to sell tickets to Date with Destiny, Unleash the Power Within, Business Mastery and things like that. During the first two weeks, I would get into the office at 9:00 and finish at 8:00 PM. Had long hours, making countless phone calls and I struggled because I focused on making the cold calls and calling people from the lists and database and had the book of contacts, it was ages ago when they downloaded that online. It was over a year or so. I pretty much had to build up my leads and some people attended the UPW, wanting to do Date with Destiny, but ultimately after many, many phone calls, I almost wanted to give up because I thought to myself, if I cannot make one sale by today and it had been two weeks, I said to myself, "If I cannot make a sale, I need to quit."

That's how I went into the office on that day and I thought to myself, if I make a sale I can stay, because tomorrow is rent day. If I don't get anything paid, I don't know how to pay my rent. I was completely broke, I had a session with one of the people that were interested in Date with Destiny. I called her up again and I continued the conversation we'd had, and it suddenly clicked. Instead of being all fluffy and talking about certain things, I listened to what she said, and I asked all the questions and after going back and forth to my supervisor asking, "Can she do this? Can she reschedule to attend Date with Destiny if she can't make it for whatever reason." "Yes." So, then I said, "Okay, now that I answered all your questions, are you ready to confirm your ticket for Date with Destiny and attend it in half a year's time?"

And she said, "Yes!" "okay, great. So, what's your credit card number?"

I was jumping up and down inside, obviously I didn't do that while I was talking to her and after I finished that conversation, I had my first sale. I just made $1,000 immediately. I was literally jumping up and down because that $1,000, it was payday the following day, so they actually paid it out to me that following day. that commission meant I had money to pay for my rent and I was so relieved. That for me, that's resilience. If I would have given up one day beforehand, that would have never happened. Now, if I would have gone, "This is not for me. I can't do this. I give up," I would not be sitting here right now talking to you about this. I would be in a job that is a 9:00 to 5:00 job and it just pays the hourly wages and that's it.

That kicked off my career in sales. From there, I made an average between five to $10,000 commission monthly during my time working for the company, turning over an additional million dollars approximately between the 12 months I was working for them. Then I got a great testimony and reference from my supervisor and got offered another job with Universal Events at the time. That's how my career started. I'm glad that I went through all of this because today I can literally talk to people about it and say, "This is what you need to do," Now, if I would have not gone through that and just smiled and learn from somebody else and then copied that, I'd not be who I am today.

Today, one of my clients had a coaching call with me and I was giving a quick call helping them getting unstuck or I said to her, "Well, you want to increase your cash flow? Talk to people that already want it, because it'll be a lot easier for you to make the sales than if you're trying to warm up the new people because selling anything over the phone that is 1,000 to 10,000 pounds or euros is a tough job, but if you've already sold to that person before something that is of value, and you remind them why they would want to be there and the experience they can get, then they're much more likely to go. Yes, here is 1,000 pounds for the event of UPW."

My thing is all about keep on going. The resilient part, is in everything that I do. So not only in my job, but also when I had Bell's palsy or when I struggled to meet my sales targets, I would keep on pushing through. I keep on going through, whatever I do, that I can do to the best of my ability to get better. These days, what I've found with people, entrepreneurs, the small business owners tend to give up too quickly. Something doesn't work out or it doesn't work. I try and then you ask, "So how long did you actually do it?" "I only did it for a week or a month." It's like, "Well, you did it for a week or a month, but have you done this, this, and this?" "Oh, no, but I really want to get to this part where the money comes in."

The money doesn't come in if you don't put in the work. If you are not resilient in following, applying yourself better and being open to apply yourself better and learn from people like myself, then you're not going to get there, and this is where I say coaches, personal trainers, even small business owners fail is at not being resilient enough to really take you from one to another to another. It's like, "Oh, I went to this seminar and learned about this program." It's Great. Then, you ask "So how's it going?" "I haven't started it yet." "But you spent 4,000 grand on it." "Yeah, but you know, I've been busy working on that...?"

The same person half a year later, "So how are you doing?" "Oh, great. I'm now doing the internet marketing." "How's it going?" "Oh, I've only tried it a little, so far, no money." They do that all the way through, and the event organizers know that and the thing about that is, I'm doing my own event, you need to follow-up with people that buy those products. You need to make sure that they make use of it, otherwise all you're doing is turning money, getting the money flowing, but you're not really serving people because they're buying a product and they're not doing anything with it.

I believe that when you are the service provider or the organizer of an event where the option is to buy a program, it is your responsibility to check in to see how they're doing so that you can be of better service next time around. So, you can always improve and even give feedback to speakers if they are not really performing at their best when they could. So, I'm a big believer in that, but you know, that is something that I want to transform into next year. So that's why I'm doing the Ultimate Entrepreneur Event.

I got one person that's coming along and she's talking about overcoming obstacles in life and business. So, an inspirational speaker. So, for me, that's resilience. All my life, even as a kid, I always thought I wanted to be an actor. It was that thing. It was like, "Oh, I want to be an actor. I want to be on the screen. I want to do this. I want to do that." I even studied it, which is teaching you all about being able to react or the other person being truthful to who you are, how you would react in that situation and emotionally being connected and all that.

I enjoyed the journey of doing all this, though I found that as an actor, I needed to only look good, do my part and shut up and I'm not that kind of person. I'm more, the person that no matter how good I look, I tell you my opinion and if you don't like it, so what? That is my approach and during camera class, the acting teacher asked everybody, "So what is your dream? Or what do you want to achieve?" I said, "Well, I'm working on a script right now. Right now, my dream, if you ask me is that I get production going with that. I get filmed and Meryl Streep would be one of the main characters playing my mom, and that'd be my dream." Because I love Meryl Streep. I think she is amazing.

Now, the mentor and acting teacher I had at the time, he thought it's time to be realistic and give me hard feedback. I asked him nicely, his name's Billy. I said, "Bill, please stop right now because you asked me what my dream is. I shared it with you. Regardless of what you think, it's not your place to tear it apart." He kept going and he kept ridiculing me about my dream and that it's not realistic, that I should dream on and I will never get there and so on. One of the other students forced me to support him. It was one of his students that hasn't reached his potential yet. He got a lot of acting jobs, but to be honest, just because you are an actor in many acts doesn't mean that you made it because seriously you don't need to get the character plays or anything like that.

So anyway, I said to everybody, "Look, I don't want to talk about it anymore," and he kept going. So, after the acting class, after the film class, I thought to myself, I was so furious. I was so angry. I felt let down. I felt like the acting teacher betrayed my trust in him and I was furious, and I went back home. The next day I had woken up and it felt just like I could not go back there. I felt sick to my stomach thinking about it and I just thought I need to stop and I just stopped with acting altogether at the time.

It wasn't stopping because of what he said, but I just realized that the bullshit politics of what other people think and you wanting them to, and again, you come back to love, I mean, if I would have just loved myself and been secure enough in myself, maybe it would have not affected me that much, but because I wanted him to be proud of me and acknowledge me and all of that, and I looked up to him, what he did affected me that deeply that it was literally sticking me in my stomach. I couldn't even go back and just forgive him, move on. I couldn't do that and hindsight, if I look back, I mean, I could have done that now, but you know, that was like ten years ago now and you learn and grow and I don't regret it because in that moment, it also made me realize I don't want to be a person that is told who they can and cannot be. I want to be my own hero. I want to be my own self and inspire and transform people's lives.

The only way that I can imagine doing that is doing what I'm doing now, writing a book, inspiring people, speaking on stage, helping people coaching, training them and sharing my story because then I can influence in a positive way millions of people around the world in what I do. If I do that on more stages, the more I can be a positive influence, inspiration and help them with their business and their own self-development and growth. For me, transformation is an ongoing thing. People talk about transformation like a onetime thing, but the reality is, no matter if you're getting better or worse, it's the transformation and in our lives, we can continue to transform. For me, transformation means continued growth, trying things out, learning new things, surrounding myself with mentors and coaches that believe in me enough to say, "You know what? Your dream is big. I love it. Go for it." Even if in the back of their minds, they go, "Oh, this guy's crazy," but they don't speak it out because they understand that is their own negative backtalk. So, for me a mentor and coach are never supposed to project their negative thoughts or their negative self-beliefs onto their students or client in any shape or form because that will stunt the growth of their students or clients.

So, if I have a certain belief and I force that belief onto you because you're paying me, then I project my own self onto you and if you take that on, I'm responsible for stopping you growing or believing that you can't grow, and the thing is, I have the responsibility not to do that. So, I need to censor myself and say, "Look. What you're sharing with me, in my eyes, it's impossible. However, if you feel you want to achieve that, here is how you can achieve that," instead of saying, "Oh, you can never achieve that, because I had a bad experience in my life." Who am I to say?

There are people out there that are living proof in life that have overcome all the obstacles and even though people, doctors, and other people tell them, "You cannot achieve it," they still did it. I am living proof that even with Bell's palsy, you can regain the movement in your face and you can heal yourself and you can rebuild your life. Even though the top doctor in Australia told me he doesn't know when it will heal. A doctor in England, when I had Bell's palsy the second time around, they told me the same kind of thing. They gave me antibiotics some eye drops and told me, "Look, you just have to wait and see."

"I knew the answer already because they're just helpless in that area." My thing that drove me to keep on going is that I want to be an inspiration to tell people with Bell's palsy, "There is hope. You can regain movement of your face and you can start smiling again." One of the reasons why I'm sharing this story is to also inspire them and to say, "Western medicine, get your freaking lazy ass up off your chair and stop projecting your limiting beliefs onto your patients. Instead, give your patients hope and find a treatment and start working with Eastern medicine to serve the patients better," because Eastern medicine, the Chinese, have all the treatments in the world, but it's almost like two separate worlds.

It's like there is Eastern medicine, acupuncture, cupping, Massages, face massages, exercises and so on to get the face muscles stimulated. Hypnosis and then there is the Western medicine that give antibiotics or anti-inflammatory eye drops and that's it. It's doesn't make sense. Well, all it really is, is an inflamed cell that doesn't translate the signals to the muscle. So, all that needs are the cell needs to heal itself and then it can start transmitting the signal again to your muscle in your face. Then it'll start working again eventually. It will take time, but the faster you start treating it and the more you do and not give up and believe in that you can do that, the more and the quicker it will heal.

I mean, one of the treatments that I did besides hypnosis was rapid transformation therapy and that was really, really empowering and I had to go past beliefs and get my past integrated to become one with me accepting that I am different and that's okay and being different, I can stand out and I can share my message with others and that helped me letting go. That work was also one of the reasons why now my face is much more in balance. So, there is no right or wrong. You just need to keep on going, be resilient and not give up in believing in yourself that you can heal yourself with assistance of other people.

That was an ongoing transformation and still a transformation because my face now I can smile. Is there a little bit more movement wanting there? Yes. So, it's still a transformation, though I'm very happy that I got my smile back and my thing that I want to tell people is, "Don't ever let anybody else tell you who you are or what you can and cannot do or what you can achieve or anything like that. Instead, take it with a pinch of salt what they tell you and then forget about it and just believe in yourself and go with what you believe in. Focus on what you want to achieve and do anything and everything that supports you in getting there, including choosing the right kind of people that are supporting you because then you can create the life that you really desire to have. No matter if it's in business or in your private life."

CHAPTER 7

The Ups & Downs of Coaching

A mentor is somebody that tells you what to do. They'll literally tell you how to go from A to Z and every step along the way. A coach is someone that challenges your point of view, and asks you questions to unlock your potential and to get you to realize what you can do when you're really focused, and really helping you redefine your belief systems and the way you think about the world around you, the way you perceive yourself to be, your own values, and who you are. The coach does that by asking the right kind of questions and guiding you along the way without necessarily always providing the answer but by asking the question that unlocks for you the answer to discover. Sometimes they ask, and they answer. Sometimes they just ask a question and let you think about it until you have a breakthrough, and then you discover what it is that you really needed to learn.

There are different coaches, different mentors out there and I think there are also different coaching styles. There's the style where it's really nurturing and being there and warm fuzzy kind of feeling you get from that coach. Then there's the coaches like big head kind of coach that tells you to step out of feeling pity for yourself. Then there is the coaching style that is literally a combination of a little bit of both. And at the same time, they use humour to lighten the mood and they get you to laugh at things instead of being strict about it. They get you to realize how silly certain things are and you laugh about it and release the stress.

Then there's the coach that is literally very, very much down to earth. They're kind of that person that allows you to unfold yourself, to really open up, so they're really supplying the space that you feel secure, and then asking questions and guide you along the way. As they ask the questions they'll tell you metaphors they'll tell you stories and makes you think differently. And then, as you're listening to them, you think about it, that's when you have a breakthrough.

I had every type of coach on this planet that you can imagine. Right now, I've got a mentor and a bit of a coach, but I'd say it's more of a coach than a mentor.

He does sometimes tell me what I need to do, but most of what he does that I am with you, with him and he's coaching me, he's asking me questions and he's telling me stories. The stories are the ones that make me think differently, that I look at things differently and have a breakthrough moment. Then he gives me tasks to do to unfold what's within me that I need to discover more about. Then the tasks I do between the sessions pull me to discover more about who I am, what I want to know about.

The problem these days though is that coaches and mentors do not need certification to be qualified. I mean it's great that when you are a coach and you've got certification, you are in the industry recognized, you've got a certification, you've got NLP and things like that. But there are no specific requirements that's given by the government or any institution for you to do your work as a coach, which makes it difficult to figure out which ones are good at it and which ones are just telling an event without it, but they're not. The same with mentors.

There are now mentors out there that literally take £3000, £4000, £5000, £10000, or even as much as £20,000 of your money, and the little time they spend with you is literally not worth that money because there's a lack of a support system for you to feel safe in being around them, in being open to them because it's so hard to reach them. It's so hard to ultimately get hold of them, you then need to make a special time to be around them and that puts a person out. But because those people are in such demand they must create those boundaries along the way. Yet, it's not necessarily supporting, the customer supporting their way to build those relationships.

Some mentors they have good intentions, but they are inexperienced in how to deal with certain personalities and expectations. As a result, their customer doesn't get the value that they paid for, and then they end up just being £3,000 to £10,000 shorter on cash not having received anything from it, and they don't get a refund from it. And the thing about that is when you are a coach or a mentor or you do both, you always need to do your best to deliver the service that they paid for. Now, if they're not willing to be coached or they're not ready to be coached and mentored and then paid you, then that's a different story. What I have an issue with though is when I'll see people paying for mentoring and coaching and the person that provides that service is not responsive, they're not getting back to the student or to the client in a timely manner, they don't take on board the feedback. There's something about having it their way or the highway, and they are not helpful. That is what I have an issue with. I think ultimately you need to be flexible with your students to a certain extent. You need to be willing to make the time and be responsive, so when the client contacts you and they need your help then get back to them in 24 or less.

Today, even when we are busy, and we are traveling there's no reason you cannot send text to the person and say, "Look, I am traveling right now, but I will be available tomorrow at this time." There's no reason ... It takes five seconds to do. That is the thing that I am really displeased about in the industry, in general, is that some coaches and mentors out there, they take us for granted. They forget that they once started from the bottom up. Now that they're doing so well instead of appreciating their customers and instead of really helping them, as soon as they got the money they'll literally leave them on the side and only look at them when it suits their timetable and otherwise, they don't care. That is not a good approach because in my experience I had at least 10 coaches or mentors that were like that in my lifetime, and that is very bad.

Out of, I'd say, at least 20 people that coached and mentored me at least half of them were bad in overcharging, under-delivering, not being responsive, not taking accountability in being willing to adjust what the outline is of what was promised and then not delivered. That is where I think, well, at least half if not more need to really have a good look at themselves and ask, "Why am I a coach and mentor? Why am I doing this? Am I really doing this because I want to serve people and really help them to elevate their life and their business and what they experience in life or am I just doing it because it's good money?" Because if it is just for you to do it for the money then stop what you're doing and stop being a coach and mentor because you, this might sound harsh, you're not deserving of being a coach and mentor if you think like that. The reason being, you need to come from a place of care and love.

You need to want to serve the people in the best possible way. Even if they are at the bottom and you are at the top, you still need to understand where they're coming from and be able to serve them at that level and then elevate their level and bring them up to your level. Then also, requires adaptability, and requires that you are being transparent, open, and caring. That also means responsive when they need you, so that is one reason why my coaching packages ... One of the things that I have is SOS calls.

If you feel stuck at some stage ... As I said once before if you're stuck and you want feedback, then text me. Feel free. I'll do a 15-minute phone call with you and I'll help you get unstuck.

I had a really great experience. That was interesting because the thing that happened at the time when I was working as a personal trainer in Australia, I felt at the time really stuck. I felt like I didn't want to be a personal trainer anymore. I didn't know what to do anymore. I felt like there must be something else out there for me to do besides personal training. What I did is I entered a fitness competition that was going on at Fitness First, and one of the prizes was win 12 sessions with a life coach. It was worth about two and a half thousand pounds or something like that, so even more than that. I entered the fitness competition and there were lots of prizes. I think there was a bicycle you could win, a holiday, and lots of different things, but I wanted to win that life coaching because I felt like I needed it the most.

I did the fitness competition, I entered it. Didn't think anything more about it, kept on working. Three weeks later, I get an email saying, "Congratulations for entering the fitness competition we would like to reward you with ... You just won the life coaching package. Please give us a call to arrange your coaching sessions." I was so excited. "Yay," first time I had won something that really meant something, so it was really, good. I called up and said, "Listen I got this email is this a joke or is this for real?" And they said, "No, no, no. it's for real." I said, "Oh, my God. I've never won anything. Thank you."

That is how I got into coaching myself, I remember the first session I had. Her name was Julia, I think. In Australia, it was in Sydney. I remember the first time we met I felt so out of place because she was all smiles and happy and full of energy, and I was totally down and totally the opposite of her. I thought to myself, in my mind, it was a prank or something because she's so freaking happy. But it was a positive experience. I had a lot of learnings from it, a lot of breakthroughs. Even understanding other people's point of view of the world because until that moment I only understood my point of the world.

When you only understand your point of the world as being it's my way or the highway, it's a very isolating way to be because you're literally isolating yourself from the world. You don't understand people when you think like that. You only see your way or that's it. From doing this, from having the life coaching sessions at 12, one of the biggest breakthroughs I had was understanding another people's perception of the world and how I can be more empathetic and understanding of where they're coming from without judging and just being accepting of it. That was a huge breakthrough for me. The other breakthrough was that I started living again. I started doing things that I enjoyed doing including acting.

I did a lot of things again that I stopped doing for a long, long, long time. As a result, I also ended up enrolling into becoming a NLP Master Practitioner. I did my training with Dr. Tad James. I mean he was a great coach and mentor to me for a while. I do believe in what he's doing. At the same time certain things, I observed later down the track that, well, that shouldn't be the case. But that was not regarding mentoring and coaching. It was more like his personal behaviour on certain subjects where when you pay 20,000 Australian dollars to do a self-development training for a week where you're invited to dinner and then you needed to pay for your own alcohol or things like that where I just sometimes questioned, well, that's just not cool. You know.

Then after that, I've done lots of different trainings. I had a JV mentor named Kerwin Rea. I learned from him how to create JVs that can complement one another. He was a great mentor for me for a while. I've worked and studied with Reframe Martin on how to sell from stage. Then I worked with one of her coaches on a regular basis and on myself. That coaching was really good, but it wasn't set up well, to be honest. In my eyes, it was way too mainstream. It could've been organized way better. But I told them about that and they were accepting of my feedback and they were also accommodating to a certain extent, and I'm grateful for that.

Then there are personal trainers that are working throughout my years that some of them are really, great, some of them less than great. They're just going through the motions. Then I had mentors and coaches like that truly made a big impact on me such as "James Heppner, Tony & Nicki Vee and Cheryl Chapman, to name a few of the outstanding ones. When I was working for other Companies we had, in-house Coaching & Training. For example, when I was working at Empowerment my supervisor was my mentor and coach. She helped me through some things. When I didn't know what to do in making sales phone calls or when I had an issue with a customer or had to deal with certain things, she helped me understand certain things where I was just able to have her as a sounding board. I'm grateful for that. That was awesome.

When I worked with Universal Events], they assigned me a private coach that trained me on how to practice my skill sets on sales. The coach would sit next to me and then listen to the conversation and then give me feedback, and I found that useful. She would come in once a week and then you'd have an hour with her, and that was paid for by the company. That was useful. At the same time, the downside of that was also that the company controlled everything you were talking about even outside of the office. So, when I was working an event and their things happening at the event that would lead back to the coach they would tell me off if it wasn't in a line with what they wanted me to think and say. That is one of the things that's a downside when a company provides you with a coach.

You cannot be 100% yourself because if you think you can, it's literally frowned upon. It's not accepted. They want you to be the ambassador of the company all the time, so you don't have a private life. You're literally on 24/7 for that company representing you. If you think that you can have a private life and follow your own dreams, think again. They will threaten to fire you and demote you and make your life miserable. Those were the reasons why I left that company because of that.

Then you take a century education, I had a mentor and a coach as my manager. She was there all the time. Whenever I needed a sounding board or had questions or wanted to have feedback she would be there as well. In my professional career, I always was surrounded by coaches and mentors, in some capacity. When I wasn't working and employed by a company and I wouldn't have a coach, I would seek out coaches and mentors that I could work with to elevate myself. That is an important factor.

One of the good coaches and mentors that I had, that delivered more than I expected, for instance, was

Tony and Nikki vee. They're both great, great people. I did the master coach certification with them last year, I think it was, and the accreditation as well. Even when I didn't have an appointment, even when we would meet at an event or spontaneously bump into each other, and they would just ask, "So how is it going, Dario? What's happening?" They would take an active interest, and then I'd tell them.

Out of the blue, they would say, "Dario, if you want why don't we have coffee and we'll just give you some feedback." Then spontaneously you're sitting in a coffee shop and they give you some feedback on what you could do, give you some tips and ideas on what you can improve. That was out of their way, that wasn't something that was expected, but they did it anyway.

I think that is an example how you need to serve people when you are a mentor and a coach and not only do it when they are paying you and you have an appointment with them. But if you run into them or if you are talking to them and you feel that there is something that they can learn from you or you can give them constructive feedback, then do it. If it's 5, 10, 15 minutes extra of your time, who cares? It will come back in tenfold in a different way. That is the thing that some coaches and mentors out there are not doing these days. That is one thing that I want people to do more of, I did it today intellectually. I had a person that wanted a call and I did talk to her and give her some ideas to look at certain things differently, and that's it. It wasn't like an appointment that we made, it was a spontaneous thing.

When I was at the effect of feeling, I wasn't being treated well and being disrespected from my point of view I felt disrespected and because at the time what happened was I was training another apprentice to become a personal trainer and I took the apprentice along to the training session and the client felt she didn't want that and as a result instead of solving it with me she ended up telling on me through the franchise so going to Fitness First's manager and I felt really treated unfairly.

Now, when I told my coach that at the time she did an exercise with me and she said, "Okay, so this is your world. You're sitting in the chair. That's your world right now. Now, I want you to come over here," so I've changed the angel. Before I was sitting, now I stood up. I was walking into a middle of a room and I was in a different place. She said, "Now, I want you to imagine in that chair is now that person that you felt treated you unfairly. Now, I want you to think about ... Put the head on of that person and think about why she acted the way she did and how did she feel at the time when that happened. Then talk to the chair as what would you tell her when relating it to her. Looking through her eyes how would you feel, and then talk to her that way."

When I looked at it through her eyes and I talked to the chair as if I were to talk to that person it made me realize that it didn't have anything to do with me it had to do with her feeling insecure. I realized that. That was a powerful way of looking at it. I never thought about that. But when you put on the head of the person that you're talking to and then you imagine in the chair that person is there and you're talking to them, it makes you look at things from a different point of view. I understand that every person is different and just because you've got your expectations doesn't mean that that person's expectation is the same.

They might have different expectations. They might see themselves differently. If you feel like you're being intimidated, or you feel insecure about yourself and there's two guys there instead of one and you feel like you cannot do the exercises because of it, of course, you feel uncomfortable. But then at the same time, that is that person's world. That was a powerful exercise that I feel is really, good to do especially if you feel like you're making it all about you and not about the other person. If you only see your world as being the victim of something, then step out of that. Then think about, well, put a head on and ask yourself if I'm going to be this person in this situation and visualize talking to the chair. Then see how they could be, what goes on for them. Now, I'm talking to them, how does that change my point of view on understanding their point of view because when you do that it will make things a lot easier.

My current coach, he said to me at one stage before I started with him what is no longer tolerable for you, what is no longer acceptable and what does that quality life look like for you? He asked me those questions and I had to really think about them. I found the hardest one was what is the quality of life for me because quality of life has a lot of meaning to me. It means being healthy, it means having lots of money, not worrying about paying the bills, it means having freedom, it means being loved and loving someone. There's a lot of things that are in quality of life.

One of the things that I've learned during the many years is if we were to let go of all the labels that we are placing on people with the judgment calls that we are making, "Oh, this person is black, this person is gay, this person is this, this person is that," then life would be so much easier if you let go of all of that. You don't need to label people. You don't need to label somebody, "Oh, they are black or they're gay or they're Muslim," or whatever. Just it's a human being, accept that. Every human being has their own needs, but we all have certain needs and wants that are very much relatable.

We all want to feel significant to a certain extent. We all want to feel loved. We wall want to feel needed. We all want to contribute in some way shape or form. And we all want to have a good life and enjoy ourselves. We all want to have happiness, to be honest. So, if you want happiness, if you want love, if you want a good life let go of labels, let go of judgment and be accepting that every human being is as different as a snowflake that comes down from heaven.

Because I mean scientist once actually looked at the snowflakes, every snowflake even though they look the same they're different. Every human being, even a twin, even an identical twin, there's a little bit of difference in them. No one is absolutely the same, no one.

It's not just from the outside it's also from the inside and the way they are looking at people, the way we perceive the world, the values that we have, the belief systems that we all have. We all have certain things that are all very much relatable to one another and then there are certain things that are very much different, or we've got a difference of opinion, and that's okay too. When we come to accept that, when we don't need everyone to say "Yes, I agree with you on everything you're saying," and we say, "Okay, well, you might have a difference of opinion on this, it's okay. And you know what, I do agree on this and this and this point," you can get along with people so much better then and you can be much more supportive.

My thing is all about ... It sounds really cliché but if I were to be a supermodel, which I'm not, and somebody would ask me what is the one thing that you want for the world or for the people, then I literally would go with World peace. Because I think if we can support, love, and accept one another as we are and just learn to accept who the person is and just respect that that's them, then there would be no war.

There would be no war, there would be no weapons of mass destruction or anything if you were to just accept the difference of religion, of cultures, and go, "You know what, it's okay that they look different, they've got different cultures." If every culture and human being loves and respects one another and is not physically abusive and not hurtful on purpose who cares what religion they have, who cares what race they are, who cares what their preferred sexuality is, it doesn't matter. What really matters is how do you interact and love and respect people in a way that is supportive and loving and in a place where you can enjoy a quality of life.

DON'T TAKE YOUR SMILE FOR
GRANTED BECAUSE ONE, NEVER
KNOWS WHEN IT MAY BE TAKEN
AWAY FROM YOU DUE TO TRAGEDY.
SO, EMBRACE YOUR SMILE EVERY
MOMENT OF YOUR LIFE TO BRING
JOY TO OTHERS.

DARIO CUCCI

CHAPTER 8

Finding My Smile Again

I have about 20 years of experience in this industry. I started my business three years ago, so even though I did it beforehand, full-time in my business I started it three years ago. I'm very different from other mentors and coaches because I've been doing it for so long and I worked my way up.

I didn't just decide to copy someone else's system, repackage it and make it my own and then say it's mine. I developed my own ultimate sales relationship system that I'm teaching and coaching people to do right now. It helps them increase their sales, improve their customer relationships, and get more clarity about how their business is serving others of purpose. That is very unique because I look at every angle from when I work with business owner, to getting new clients, to serving your existing clients at a higher level, and have conflict resolutions to really solve issues when people aren't happy.

Some mentors and coaches out there they don't even go near that because they're too scared. They are not experienced enough to do it, so they don't even go there. Because conflict resolution or doing retention work or handling people with complaints is a different skill altogether, and not many people know how to do that. With me, you're pretty much getting everything. I even say to my clients, "Look, if you feel like you need life coaching, you don't need to go to a life coach. I am here. I am experienced in it. I've been doing this for a long, long time, so we can actually work on that."

Of course, as I done my NLP Certification, even when sales and Customer Service is my expertise is my niche. Because that's my niche, that doesn't mean I can't do the other thing if it's needed. It's just not what I'm focusing in promoting out there. What makes me different is my adaptability and my level of experience, and the reason I got that is because I worked my way up instead of just working for a few years and then saying, "I'm a coach." No, I became the coach and mentor that I am today because of my journey that got me here.

That is what makes me unique because when you come as say, a business with 10 to 15 employees, for instance, I know what to do. You come as a one-man show with a few employees, I know what to do. The only thing that I don't know what to do in that sense, I never worked with huge corporations. That is not my experience, but that is not what I'm aiming for anyway. Unless the corporation wants me to have to train their staff to motivate them and give them sales tools and strategies to get them back on track. I can do that even in corporations. But if you were to hire me for a corporation to look at the legal systems in place for sales retention and all that stuff, I wouldn't know where to start because that's not what I experience. That's the reason I don't do it.

That all makes it different in that helps via that adaptability and responsiveness that I have these days. I'm one of the only coaches and mentors that I personally know of, but I know a lot of coaches and mentors, that is as responsive as I am. You are texting me on Facebook, "What's up? Email me," whatever.

Most of the time, I get back to you within an hour. If I'm busy and I'm traveling it might take 24 hours. Other coaches and mentors out there in the industry, without naming names, take anywhere between one day to seven days to reply to an email. My last mentor from the UK, when I'd texted him he sometimes texted me back within two or three days if I was lucky. Sometimes he didn't text me back at all. Then I needed to email. Then when the assistant would call. Well, when would it be suitable for you? I needed to email that back. Then maybe two or three days later I would hear back from the assistant and not from the mentor.

If I was lucky enough to get some feedback on my PowerPoint, he would get back to me maybe at times it'd been one to two weeks. Sometimes not at all. With me, you don't have that. With me, I'm looking at the stuff that you send me. I will give feedback immediately as quick as I can. If I'm busy, I will tell you that it will take longer than just today. But I will let you know in 24 hours. That also makes me unique because quite a lot of times what our problem is some coaches and mentors just don't have the system in place to be responsive. Instead of being responsive they are reactive. What I mean by that is they are victims to their own circumstances of not being able to manage their time well, so they're all over the place and they forget to do it. As a result, their clients get unhappy because they feel not looked after. But the reason that happens is because it just overlaps that way.

I am overlapped that way, so one thing that I do with all my clients is always give them structure in how they can communicate better with their existing clients to be of better service.

What makes me smile? I think I'm very grateful that I am now at a place where I came to accept myself as I am, my absolute acceptance. I think it took me a long time to get here. But now what makes me smile is to just be myself and not to censor my thoughts or censor what I feel or anything like that. Just be myself and openly share it with people. That's pretty much it. I think that, and my sense of humour comes out when I talk and when I present. So, I'd say what makes me smile is when I hear people acknowledging what I do has helped them to have a breakthrough too. Because in my eyes that's the biggest reward for me besides the money, is also that I hear people say, "You really helped me improve my business. I'm grateful for that," or, "Because of what you shared with me, I now make more sales. And I have more clarity and I feel like a I have a better purpose in life." Those things make me smile.

The money is good. It pays the bills, but ultimately, it's all about that. Recently I've been to "making the news" and being awarded the Stardust Award, and I won it. It made me smile because of how, deeply appreciated I was and to see what I have accomplished this far. It's nice to be acknowledged. Just getting something like that makes a huge impact to me in the way of gratitude, "Thank you so much for acknowledging it." Because for a long, long time I felt no matter what I did, I had to work double hard and I didn't get any recognition. There were other people that did little to do what I did that did in comparison, they made one seminar maybe a year. I did six seminars in a year, but they got all the recognition and the publicity. And I'm like, "Well, why is that?"

Now, I don't compare myself to others anymore. I just do my thing. If people don't want to work with me, they don't like me the that's okay too because in my eyes some people are just not meant to work with me, they're not ready to work with me. To come to accept that, that's a thing as well. You need to be willing to accept that some people are just not ready to work with you yet. They might never be because I want to work with certain people that are wanting to become their own heroes in their life.

I want to enable entrepreneurs to really get their message out there and build their business. And not only make sales but in making sales also gain a seller reputation working with me because of the way they're looking out for their customers because of learning from my experience and knowledge. There are some certain criteria I always say for everybody for me to work with them.

When you go horse riding, for instance, if you go horse riding you need to be willing to go onto the saddle and get prepared for it and do what is required to control the horse. If you're not willing and not coachable to listen to what the trainer tells you to do with the horse, and you're just trying your own thing, eventually you will fall off the horse. Okay, the horse will throw you off. Then you need to be willing to give back into this level and keep on going. But if you're not the person that is willing to be coached and trained, the same thing will keep on happening. So, horse riding isn't for everybody. Right?

Same for coaching and mentoring. It's not for everybody because if you're not willing to listen and apply what you learn, then you will keep falling off, you will keep on failing, you will not actually get there, and eventually, you might give up. The people that I want to work with is people that are willing to get into the coaching zone as I call it, and be willing to be coached and mentored and taken on board just as they would if they were to go to learn horse riding. They're going to think, "Okay, so the trainer tells me to really get into the saddle and really hold on to the horse. And then there are certain movements that I need to make with my hands to guide the horse. I'm going to do that, and I'm going to listen to the trainer." The same as if I coach, you need to listen to the coach and to the mentor to succeed and not trying to prove to them that you know better.

Those people that think like that, they will never get anything out of coaching and mentoring. That is the reason why I'm okay if some people are going, "Well, I'm not ready to coach yet." And I go, "Okay, cool," whereas if I would've gotten that objection 10, 15 years ago I most likely would've tried to convince them to be ready. Even up to three years I would've don't that.

What I've learned during the last three years is I don't do myself any favour as a coach and mentor when I try to convince some because it will backfire. I might try to go, "Look, this is the price. This is the package. This is how we work together. Yes or no?" And if they say, "Yes," great. If they say, "No," I don't do objection handling that much. I give them a couple of re-frames to have them think, but then I'll leave it because I know that if they're not taking accountability to change nothing is going to change.

Even them paying me the money that they're paying me will not change it. They will not make use of it.

I've had coaching classes like that, and I don't want coaching classes like that. Keep your money, and then I'll work with somebody that is willing to do the work to get the results because I want to stand out. I want people to talk about the results that they're getting to work with me instead of working with people just for the money. Them not getting results because they feel like they don't want to do the work to get there.

SHANNON CUNNINGHAM
PERSONAL TRAINING

Shannon Cunningham is a health and wellness expert. A graduate in Human Movement Education from the University of Sydney, he has over 20 years of international experience in the fitness industry.

He is determined, focused and straight-talking. His passion is to help as many as possible to reach and maintain optimal health and fitness.

Shannon has helped people with:

- Mindset

- Fitness

- Nutrition

This has enabled thousands to get into improved physical shape, and to feel totally empowered.

Just commit to expending the time and effort and Shannon will ensure you meet, beat and exceed all of your personal health goals.

Get started NOW and book your Bespoke Online Personal Training Package with SC/PT™ to achieve your Health & Fitness Goals.

DECISIONS. ACTIONS. RESULTS.

113

If you are looking to improve your Business, Sales Revenue & Customer Service. Then get in touch with me to organize your first Complimentary Consultation.

I help Business Owners with:

- Re-Programming of The Mindset
- Sales & Customer Service Communication
- Business Strategies & Structure

To enable them to improve their Business, increase their Sales Revenue and gain a stellar Reputation for their outstanding Customer Service, after having worked with me.

Visit: www.dariocucci.com

to get in touch with me.

Dedication

I like to dedicate this Book to those that
have helped me gain Clarity & find my Way in Life.
As it is a very personal
Journey that I share with everyone that reads this
Book.
Thank you Mum & Dad for always being there for
me, even during the toughest
of Times in my Life, without you I would
not have been able to have the courage to be as
Honest and open as I have been in writing this Book.
I also, like to thank Cheryl Chapman for reaching out
to me and helping me with winning my Smile back
by holding RTT
(Rapid Transformation Therapy) to heal my Bells
Palsy.
Besides all of that I like to also dedicate this Book to
Andy Harrington, that has provided me with the
guidance,

knowledge, connections and Wisdom to become a better Public Speaker to

inspire others with the Message I share, so that I can have a bigger positive

impact in the World by reaching more People as a Keynote Speaker.

And last I like to dedicate this Book to all the People out there that suffer or have

suffered from the horrible Disease called "Bells Palsy" to never give their Hope that one Day "You Can Smile Again"!

Don't let the Doctor's tell you, your Destiny, do whatever it takes to heal your Body & Mind, to choose your own Destiny & win your Smile back!

Yours Truly

'DON'T TRY TO BE AVERAGE
AND FIT INTO THE CROWD.
DO YOUR BEST TO BE
OUTSTANDING AND
STAND OUT!'

DARIO CUCCI

Printed in Great Britain
by Amazon